Introduction.

Hi, My name is Liam Campbell, at the time of writing this, I am 22 years old. I am born and raised in Glasgow. I have 2 parents, 4 Siblings, 2 Nephews and 1 Niece, and a beloved Dog.

Up until I was 15, my life was ~~  dn't do much with myself until I ⁓g instantly. With Meeting f ll across the UK, I have fou

None of this would have I ⁓ak Young Peoples Theatre, A ... to Glasgow young peoples. 1 ⁓⁓ wonderful things and continues to have the kids ⁓⁓ interest at heart.

Aside from theatre, I work at a residents centre in the heart of the North-East of Glasgow. Barmulloch Community Development Company. Working here has been a life changing experience: Being connected with the community, Meeting thousands with fascinating stories and being proud that I can call this place my home. BCDC does an immense amount to help those in the community and they have helped me in more ways than I can count.

Lastly, I want to thank you everyone that has a copy of this book, It means a lot to me. Enjoy.

Thanks to:

My Family, Toonspeak, BCDC, Friends, Isabella Dorta and Lauren Gillespie, Myself and Of course... My Stargirl.

Like her mum

I'm sorry But I don't Want To be a Poet,
Thats not My Purpose,
I don't Want to beat around the Bush.
I want to tell you how things are and how they make
me feel.
Thats all anybody wants I think. to be able to just say anything
without caution
or consequence.
so, I'm not a poet, I'm an actor
So that's what I'm going to do, I'm just going to talk about me and my life.
My name is Liam Campbell.
I'm from the northeast of Glasgow.
I'm 21 years old
I am single
I like my family, friends a lot and apparently people that are listening while I talk
but there was only one girl in this world, I love and care for more than anything
and she's gone,
I loved her so much and in some people's eyes
she was just an abundance of cells
and hey maybe she was, but she was MY abundance of cells, the most precious
clump of atoms I've ever known.
she would be 4 right now and her name would be Elamay, she would be beautiful
and smart, she'd have dark hair and big dark eyes just like her mum,
and she would be my daughter.
and that's where this dream ends. Thats the only thing that makes me upset
anymore,
everything else is but a fleeting moment until the thought of days
I could have with her at Murdock country park and Kelvingrove art gallery.
so
I'm sorry but I don't want to be a poet, that's not my Purpose, I don't want to beat
around the bush.
I want to tell you how things are and how they make me feel.
Thats all anybody wants I think. to be able to just say anything without caution or
consequence.
I'm not a poet, I want to be a father
So that's what I'm going to do, I'm just going to talk
about
her, my life
Elamay Rose Campbell
she is from Glasgow,
she is 4 years old
And I care and love for her so fucking much, I would do anything for her.
and she's not even here

A Scarecrows duty

I don't love you; I never have.
I could one day, I kind of hope I do
one day. For now, no
but I am loyal to you.
you can say you love someone
and also hate them.
kill them with kindness.
keep your friends close,
and your enemies closer
loyalty is a promise,
its a duty, an oath.
no deception, no crossing fingers,
no April fools joke
from the moment I saw those stargirl eyes,
I swore that oath to be loyal to you.
to cherish you, to make you happy in every way possible.
I haven't told you this because I don't want to scare you off,
so, I show you.
by pushing the hair out of your eyes and behind your ear.
by kissing your forehead, whenever I have to leave.
by bringing a hoodie, I know doesn't match my outfit but I bring it in case your cold on
our first non-date date .
you mean so fucking much to me,
I don't think you even know,
it doesn't seem enough,
I don't want to do too much
where you think I'm being too clingy
but not so distant you think I'm not interested.
for fuck sake id go to Glasgow uni for 4 years,
and get that dreadful accent I'm that interested in you.
I want to know your favourite movie,
I want to know what Spotify wrapped genre you got in November,
mine was the vampire by the way.
I want to know about your family.
and what words you don't like the sound of.
I don't like the word cream, or what cream is,
I always except it to be sugary but its just white water.
its so difficult writing a heart felt poem coz I always go off on a tangent
but that's how it feels when I think of you. unpredictable and amazing
who knows maybe after tonight you will tell me what words you don't like.
or maybe you'll tell me that I have scared you off.
either way, its a pleasure to know you, romantically or from now on, not
I have only ever wanted to be honest with you, and I have been from the moment we met.
the only thing I've kept from you till now is how I feel.
I just hope that moment doesn't end here

Mold, an Oven and some white vinegar.

when you're in love, do you imagine
in your head this dream house, with your dream living room,
dream pet and even a favourite oven.
I had in my mind a base of all our memories,
a memory palace you like. Of our date nights, our sleepovers, our fall outs, our makeups everything. and the oven is there too
well, I found Mold yesterday.
and you weren't there to tell me what to do,
so, I used my dumb guy brain, and I phoned my dumb guy friend and he said put bleach on it
I wanted to get your opinion, but you weren't answering so I put bleach on it, and while it was good yes, it killed the Mold, yes
something else replaced it. yes
fungus.
      A toxic combination of Mold and bleach
I panicked again, so, I again
phoned my dumb guy friend and he didn't know what to do, so he left, and you never came home,
the fungus is consuming everything,
its consuming the walls,
the couch,
you alone could fix it,
save us and our palace
it's all gone now, all that's left is fungus and sadness
it's been 2 years, the fungus had taken our palace and our Oven,
and now I have a new palace.
with new memories,
a new queen and an air fryer that I'm too sacred of to use so I use the microwave.
and I find Mold.
again.
I stare and it stares back, I look away because staring is rude
then I remember it's not a person so its fine
I rush to tell the new queen of the palace and she says use white vinegar.
it kills the Mold but it won't kill you. she says
So I trust her for some reason and sprayed some white vinegar,
left the room for 10 minutes and came back and it was gone.
but you weren't there.
the Mold is gone
so why aren't you back and why being the oven back.
I know how to fix what went wrong just come home.
we can remove the fungus
we can have our palace back.
we can chuck the air fryer and get the oven back
where are you,
I need you,
please come home.
Please

Just be Happy

In a world fixated on purpose and objective,
there's something
liberating
about bathing in the pure joy
for simply being happy.
It's like finding a secret garden hidden within the chaos of life,
Of building crashing and false gods being revered
where the flowers bloom just for the sake of blooming,
not because they're expected to do anything.
Happiness,
in its most genuine form,
needs no justification, no end goal to validate its existence.
for I exist solely for the sake of myself.
When you embrace happiness without purpose, it becomes addictive
spreading like wildfire through the heart of you.
reaching out to others, clinging on for dear life
It's the kind of happiness that doesn't seek to achieve anything
it merely radiates from within, touching lives in ways you may never fully
comprehend.
It's the smile you share with a stranger on the street, the laughter that echoes through a room,
the warmth that fills the spaces between us, connecting us, touching us.

Infectious Joy

In a world that often measures success by material or wealth or social status,
finding joy in the simple moments can feel more so,
It's about finding peace
here and now,
in the beauty of a sunset,
the sound of groan tube, those things that go,
It's about recognizing that
happiness
isn't something to be chased or acquired.
it's something to be embraced
and shared freely,
with no strings attached.
we are not the puppeteers of other peoples happiness,
So let us revel in the sheer delight of being alive,
of experiencing the full spectrum of human emotions,
without the pressure to constantly
strive for something bigger than yourself.
Without feeling like we have the power to dictate others lives
Let us embrace happiness for its own sake,
allowing it to weave its way into the fabric of our lives,
colouring every moment with its technicolour hues.
one smile at a time.
one hug at a time
one handshake at a time
one kiss at a time
And let us remember that in sharing our happiness with no purpose,
we create a ripple effect of positivity that has the power to transform the world.

Not about sunflowers

In the quiet solitude of the night,
I find myself lost
in you,
my heart is like a bed of flowers,
illuminated by the glow of the moon.
Your presence,
like a gentle breeze on a summer's night,
stirs something within me, awakening a longing that defies reason.
I've always believed that love is like
a flower,
its petals unfurling eagerly under
the warm embrace of the sun.
But with you,
it's as if I'm witnessing the impossible,
watching as those same flowers bloom under the tender caress of the moonlight.
You see, my love for you is like those flowers,
reaching for the light even in the darkest of nights.
It's a love that defies logic, that thrives in the shadows
and blossoms under the watchful gaze of the moon.
And yet,
just like
the impossibility
of flowers blooming under moonlight,
the idea of you loving me back
feels equally impossible.
It's a notion that I've long dismissed
as nothing more
than a fleeting dream,
a fantasy too beautiful to be real.
But perhaps,
just like those moonlit flowers, there's a hidden magic
within us, a resilience that defies
the odds and dares to believe
in the impossible.
And so, as I stand
beneath the stars,
my heart a field of lunar flowers,
I can't help but wonder
if maybe,
just maybe,
our love
is destined to bloom
against
all
odds.

Part I

Love defies reason.
Love isn't about a list of categories or boxes that they tick.
Love connects two people because it simply does.
But for you,
My sweet, love has not been kind.
Great kings and gods have borne witness.
of your body and your talents.
And you fall in love.
But they do not hold your hand and land with you.
You watch as they love another,
It turns you dark, it turns you cruel,
And you turn them to monsters,
revealing they're true forms for all to see,
But don't fret,
One day you will love again,
One day you will see me as I have watched your story unfold,
And Love
Love will defy reason once more.

Who I think I am

I think
I have mastered the art
of appearing stupid,
of weaving tales that draw laughter and concern.
But it's all a facade,
a mask carefully crafted to conceal the contents within.
In truth,
I'm just a quiet observer,
lost in the labyrinth
of my own thoughts,
collecting data
yearning for solitude
amongst the endless abyss
of social interaction.
People mistake
my deep gaze for dumb fondness,
my solitude for information overload.
They believe that beneath the surface
lies nothing but emptiness,
a void devoid
of knowledge or comprehension.
I've become skilled at playing the part,
at wearing this cloak
of being the person that needs answers
as a person that has the answer
hiding myself from the eyes of denial.
But every joke I crack, every story I tell,
only serves to deepen the chasm
between who I am and who you perceive me to be.
As the reason of laughter fading into the background,
I'm left alone with my thoughts,
Longing for someone to see passed this façade and actually say
"Show them who you really are."

We will always

I will never say "I love you".
    Even though I do
I will never want to hug you.
    For I will never let go.
I will always be kind of gay.
    To throw you off my scent
I will always smile when you're near,
    But you'll never know it's because of you.
I will cherish every moment,
    When that moment is the image of you.
I will support you in your dreams,
    While silently wishing you'd notice mine.
And I will always write.
    So you can read this one day.
And you will stumble upon my letters,
    And realize they were all for you.
You will notice the longing in my eyes,
    And understand it's directed at you.
You will hear the tremble in my voice,
    When your name escapes my lips.
You will feel the weight of my unspoken words,
    Hanging heavy in the air between us.
You will sense the depth of my devotion,
    As it spills out in unexpected moments.
And finally comprehend my love for you
I mean it's been obvious.
Hasn't it?

Lets Restart

Okay, you want an answer? Here it is.
I love you I need you; I want you.

And I feel embarrassed for you, but also jealous,
That you have to someone to say this about you
And I don't even know you yet,
But I have this pure physical desire to be with you,
to pick you out of the crowd right now
and have my way with you.
to know every inch of your being.
It's been a long journey, of heartbreak and misfortune, and now that I've found you,
I don't want to look away and I can't let you slip away.
I want you to stand here with me
I want to hold you close to me
to feel your heartbeat against mine,
to feel your breath on my ear as you say my name
to lose myself in the warmth of your embrace.
I want to explore every curve of your body,
to trace the outline of your lips with my fingertips,
to taste the sweetness of your kiss.
To feel your fingers run through my hair
I know it sounds crazy, to feel this way about someone I barely know. But when I look at you, I see more than just a stranger in a crowd. I see a connection, a spark that ignites something deep within me.
You asked a simple question, but it is far from having a simple answer
all I can say is
I love – I need – I want – there isn't any poetry –
There is no structure that can make any sense of this
Only I love you, I need you and I want you

Only Human

Everyone, and I mean everyone,
has their eyes fixated on her words and her body.
reducing her to nothing more than
a hollow vase with cool tattoos.
And It pisses me off!
Do you have any idea?
how frustrating it is to
watch as you stare at her,
create fantasies of her,
but never bother to scratch beneath the surface?

You're so entranced.
with her outer beauty
that you fail to recognize
the depth of her character,
the power of her intellect,
the fierceness of her spirit.

And I'll be honest, I'm only human.
I've been guilty of it too.
Of falling into the trap of her beauty
fixating on Aphrodite's body.
But I've learned, albeit slowly,
to see beyond the surface.
To admire her quirks,
her daily rituals.
It's a conscious effort,
a choice I've made to delve deeper,
to appreciate her for more
than just her body.

So, while I'm no god myself,
I strive to see the goddess for who she truly is,
beyond the veil of her enchanting curves
and flawless stretch marks.
But on God
I wont lie to you
She is bloody beautiful.
Inside and out

The Double Helix of Love

When I think of the love I have for you
I don't know where to begin
From the first moment when I saw her,
emerald eyes gleaming with innocence,
etching themselves
into the depths of my memory
like a tattoo on my heart.
she reminds me of it every year
with a simple Snapchat memory,
a fleeting glimpse into the past that feels like a lifetime ago.
From that moment

Little did I know then that in that moment,
My life and hers would become intertwined, like two strands of DNA
together yet always separate.
Forever crossing paths
but never quite walking side by side.
Making her smile became my mission, my purpose, my duty.
Like a scarecrow, guarding the field of love

Or
when she shivered from the cold,
and without a second thought, I presented Her
my hoodie, and I just stood there
and watched
how effortlessly beautiful she was, she is.
In that moment, as I watched her enveloped in my warmth,
I glimpsed a future where we were together,
where every gesture was filled with love and tenderness.

You and I went out
on our first non-date date.
Ive seen you grow up into this beautiful, fierce but gentle dove.
But this time,
I am no scarecrow, standing stiff and lifeless in the field of love.
This time, I am ready
to spread my wings and take flight and be a dove with you.

Tastes Like…

I've always been a picky eater.
Maybe not a picky eater but I like what I like.
If I like it, I will eat it to my heart's content.

Did you know:
6 eggs and an orange can give you all the vitamins and minerals you need for a whole day.
I like eggs, eggs are sweet, so are oranges but they have seeds, and I don't like not knowing the textures of my foods.
Its not just foods, I'm picky with my drinks too.
I like my whiskeys, they're sweet also.
I don't like spirits, they're to straight forward.
I want temptation, I want desire, I want seduced.

My taste in you is personal.
It's undefined, indescribable.
It makes me feel foolish,
How can someone so particular with food not know the taste of they're favorite
Well person to eat.

Part II

And you told me your name was Paris,
I don't know you yet, but I can already tell,
You are dangerous.
Behind those soft lips is a silver tongue waiting to strike.
Oh, how dangerous you are
My soul beats something fierce for you,
a feeling so profound it engulfs,
my very being.
But there is a shadow behind you.
not of your own
Taunting this consuming passion
Revealing a haunting truth,
– that you,
my sly fox, are also my eventual downfall.
It's a paradox,
To want to love someone so deeply,
knowing that their presence in your life
could be your undoing.
Yet, despite this knowledge,
I cannot help but surrender myself to the intoxicating,
Allure for your compassion.
For every moment, we share from now on,
there's a whisper of impending tragedy in the air.
I can see it in the stars.
Written for all of time
Oh, how exciting

Devotion

I don't love her
However —
I couldn't live with myself
if after the dust has settled
she asks to have me back.
and I couldn't say yes

The waves of you

You had me submerged. In the depths of your body of water,
Gasping for air I was being overwhelmed by the waves of your skin
Slowly losing myself I would reemerge,
seeing the beauty of others that is beyond the horizon of you
but the touch of someone you love is better than admiring what I could have.
So, I go down… again
Allowing you suffocate me all over again
to consume me in your being,
for me, to consume your being
the cycle just does not end.

Male validation

You are beautiful, your heart is golden, and your eyes are starlight.
But that's not your fault.
You cant have a ponytail because it makes you convenient
But that's not your fault.

They say your worth is in the eyes of the beholder,
Judged by choices you never chose.
You dress for you
Yet whispers say you're seeking validation that way.

From the outside, I see the eyes you carry,
In a world that demands you conform and be wary.
As a spectator, I struggle with the irony presented,
That your joy is questioned, your happiness resented.

Why not wear your hair in a ponytail, wear that low cut dress, and smile with pride,
Let your heart guide you, not this twisted yellow brick road.
For beauty, my darling, is not in their validation,
But in the truth of who you are, your perfection.

Because It's easier said than done, isn't it?
To stand up tall, When the world is eager to see you crumble.
To ignore the comments, the judgments, the stares,
And live your truth.
What a world we live in.
Defined by his validation.

Man Enough

I've told you countless times before that I don't love her
But I am
Enough to admit I'm still attached.
Enough to admit I miss her.
Enough to admit I haven't deleted her photos.
Enough to admit I still read our old messages.
Enough to admit I still cry over her.
Enough to admit I still need her, and she will always have a place in my heart.
Enough to admit she deserved better than me.
Enough to admit that if she gave me another chance and I would take it without hesitation. Enough to admit watching her move on in real time hurts.
I treated her horribly and I'm sorry for that.
I never Physically hurt her, I don't have a bone in my body to do harm,
but what I did do - was allow her to love me,
when I didn't have a bone in my body,
just a hollow me and a hollow heart where she was

A love like torture

I want to be loved
I'm not desperate to be loved
I'm not begging for it
I'm not in a rush to be loved
but I would love to love
and be loved
I would love to find that person that I'm attached to by a string
I would love to hug somebody and know that they care for me
That they love me and its consistent
I would love to come home and have somebody there
just to talk to on that level
the level that you don't know if you should,
so you shake a little,
but you keep going cause it may be worth it.
I would love to do nice things for somebody
I would love to find my lobster
So we can walk around this world of a fish tank together interlinked
I would love for somebody to consider me and think about me
and care for me and worry about me
I just want to experience love again
Patience is a virtue only so few have the pleasure of having
I have it, and its not a fucking pleasure
It's torture and it's love.

A brief moment of sobriety

"Never trust how you feel about your life after 21:00 PM," is the quote I saw.
I look at the clock; it is 21:04 PM.
I know I should not trust this
heaviness
that just dropped to the pit of my stomach.
I have felt it before,
and last time I made it out alive
by putting my foot to the pedal and focusing on the drive.

I look at the clock and its now 21:13pm,
the midnight is like shadow people in the corners of my eyes.
Taunting, tempting me to do unforgivable things.
They stretch and twist the truth
make mountains out of molehills,
turning worries into insurmountable fears.
They play tricks on a weary mind,
promising clarity while delivering only confusion.

And I wake up clear of these temptations,
Mountains are now piles of clothes on the chair
And I have no fear of the dark no more
You aren't a fear anymore
And this mind has no confusion,
It's made itself up

And in a moment of habit,
I remember an idea someone had
Of making numbers to make sense of the world
And then another idea of using these numbers
No need for stars, no need for sundials
I shall make time, I shall make a clock
And I see this invention
And its 21:18pm

Part III

Listen closely now,
For I shall speak of my newfound romance,
Like the goddess of love and beauty,
In her mortal and true form.
We've all heard tales.
Of her unparalleled heart,
Her radiant beauty that turns heads
Her Captivating curves with effortless grace.
But have you truly tried to see beyond the surface,
Beyond the embellished stories spun for poets and artists.

Oh Paris, my sweet, sweet Paris,
You are a figure of myth and legend,
I often do pause to ponder the depths of your being,
To truly understand the essence of your existence
You simply take my breath away.

Yes, she may inspire.
distant glances and sighs of admiration,
but she is also so much more,
she is a catalyst for artistry and expression.
Yet, in your haste to admire her beauty,
you overlook the strength that lies within her,
the resilience forged in the fires of her heart.

For she has faced heartaches and betrayals,
just like any of us.
And yet, she endures,
her spirit unbroken,
And her mind unwavering.

To the girl that gets to love him next
(Collab with Lauren Gillespie)

He says he likes his tea with two sugars
But I know better, he likes 2 and a half

He sleeps on the left side of the bed
And has to, has to have cold pillows
He goes to the bathroom before bed so use this to flip them

When he gets back he will want back scratches
So keep your nails long,
I did this so you should too

His tattoos are his story
Remind him of the journey he took
And He takes pride in his hair everyday
So say your proud of him for these everyday

Everyday I told him I love him
Everyday I added the sugar, I scratched his back, I flipped the pillows, I Admired his tattoos and hair

I did all of this, and It wasn't enough
I wasn't enough
I hope, for his sake,
you will be

Yours Truly,
The boy that got to love him before

Alright, Einstein.

The definition of insanity is repeating an activity over and over and over and over
and over, expecting a different outcome
And it was different this time
not in a good way, but different.
every other time before this.
I would keep going. I would say
it's only one more it's fine, I'm fine.
every single time I craved that numb feeling.
Thinking that giving my love was being in love

I don't want to feel you ever again.
I don't want to hold you as you cry over him
I don't want to know what it is to love you
I don't want to feel numb again

But what if its different next time..?

Forced Evolution

I do not fear that you will see me again
Because you wont
Not the me that you knew
You will see a product of metamorphosis
A product of evolution and heartbreak
But that's what you wanted anyway wasn't it?
For me to change? To lose my muchness

I fear that you will see
the pain I have went through
in these desolate eyes
and say sorry as though
who I am now isn't who I should be
or isn't what you intended when you spun me like pottery
diluting me with food to make me soft
and pressing on my bumps and cracks
to create this empty vase
you call regret

Therapy

The good thing about we creatives is we share commonality:
A want to share how we feel
But that's the hardest part, to say how we feel so plainly
So we make these poems, these canvases, these songs and plays to convey how we feel

But go on this journey with me for a moment
If your feeling some negative way
I want you imagine what shape would it be?
Mines would be a sphere

And now give this feeling a size and where is it in the room
For me, it's just above my head, floating like the size of a Grand piano

And if your feeling had a colour would it be?
This piano sized sphere is like a dark grey for me
Now I want you to name it,
Like those people who don't call their cats whiskers, but call it Kevin or something
Mines will be called, Alex

If Alex was a thought, they would say your alone,
why don't you give up finding love
why do you feel the need to want to care for someone
what do you think your thought would say,
and what does that mean you care about
For me it means I have a lot of empathy and I value those around me

what would you have to not care about for this to go away
I'd have to not care about you, you reading or listening to this.
But fuck not doing stuff purely for other people, that's what makes me happy

And I will take Alex with me everywhere,
Proving them wrong by making people happy
So, fuck you Alex
No matter how Alex I felt.

Praying on the dead

When I see people making a wish on a star
I feel sorry for them
They don't know that the star is millions of years ahead of us
And its dead, your too late to make that wish and that too is dead

No matter how dead the stars are I still wish
Still wish for a life where I got that acting job
Still wish for those tickets to see the reboot of star wars

Still wish that my school report is good
So my parents get me a McDonalds
Maybe Life isn't all about facts and numbers,
Maybe it is just a game of chance
that's been around since those dying stars
and they're trying to help us

Rooting for us before we get our roots planted.
Or perhaps they wish upon us
What would those genies millions of years away wish for
When you have all the money in the world what do you buy
What would a god do when all the verbs exist because of them
Maybe all they want is a McDonalds too

Arts and Crafts

Religion is an odd thing
It's beautiful but it's also brought so much pain
Now I'm not religious in anyway,
I can't believe something that big, that defines the universe
made the universe because what if its wrong.

But I have faith,
I have faith there is something
or someone out there
who is proud of their school art project,
they titled "Universe"

I admire those who have faith in religion
Its like walking through a blind tunnel
not seeing the light but still going
cause you know tunnels don't last forever

Part IV

You see, it's a curious thing when you find yourself drawn to someone who is still entangled in another's embrace. I've never been one for matters of the heart. Here in the underworld, emotions are often muted, buried beneath the weight of responsibility. But her presence is a beacon of light in the darkness, a reminder of everything I've yearned for but believed unattainable.

Yet, in the presence of beauty, the air is charged with possibility. It's as if the darkness itself is lighter when she's nearby. I've never dared to hope for more. To desire... connection. But Paris is a force unto herself, a contradiction to everything I thought I knew.

She's caught in a dance of loyalty and duty. Your heart, lingering elsewhere. Tied to someone you left behind someone who fills your thoughts even in this place.

I understand loyalty. I know duty. But to yearn for one who cannot be reached... it's a torment I never foresaw. But I hear it, Paris. Your thoughts chasing another, to him. Your heart remains tethered to a past that lingers in your every glance, your every sigh.

Bound by duty, I must let her go. To ask her to stay would be selfish to her — Olympus to me. My love deserves a love free from shadows. Yet, I find myself wanting her light in this desmoterion. Though impossible, her presence stirs something deep within. I must release her to the sunlit world she belongs to.

For now, I watch, silently longing, as she tends to his pomegranate tree above—a reminder of life, of vibrancy that I can only glimpse from below. When her creations die, I welcome them as a taste of her - a gift from the goddess herself. But perhaps one day she will die in their place, and I will taste her, ripe and sweet, then I might dare to believe a different fate.

Paris, there's a weight on my heart that I can no longer carry in silence. When I first saw you in the fields above, surrounded by the blossoms of spring, something stirred within me—a longing I thought had been extinguished in this world of shadows and echoes.

I don't ask for your love freely given, for I know the complexities that bind us. But I long to know where I stand in the chambers of your heart. Am I merely a shadow in the background of your heart's landscape, cast aside in favour of memories and unfulfilled promises?
Can there be space for me among the echoes of another?

Un-Hinge

Organically is how I want love
I want it natural, to find someone
that isn't on a screen
showing the best of themselves

I want to see you through the looking glass
in those brief moments of sobriety
where life is not deluded
with fantasies and expectations

From the beginning, I want to give myself fully and freely,
not expecting a reward or a thank you,
but in hopes you would do the same
I just want someone who chooses me
over everyone else, under any circumstance.

Stargazing

I see you
I try push you away
but you keep coming back

you look at me with such gaze
with those stargirl eyes
but all I have is the fear of accidental hand holding

I'm hoping this feeling is temporary
I'm hoping i wake up tomorrow with a new fixation
that you will become a memory, a fad

But what if...
I fell for you and you reached for my hand
and
say it wasn't accidental
you meant it,
you want it
and now you got it
you got me and I got you

Gameboy

Is that really all it takes
One long conversation on a couch

I'm not mad it's not me
But I can't help feeling jealous
Watching you sink into the couch talking to him after 1 day

Sorry, I never got told
Was there a secret code
Consisting of ups and downs
Consisting of A's and B's

I'm not saying I would have used it
I'm not saying you don't have a choice who you sink for

But I've been sinking on this couch for so long
And no ones there pushing my buttons
Quite like you do

Unfinished

Some things are left better unsaid I think
So I'm going to write about it

I love you
No
I have always loved you, in more ways than you can count

And you say you love me too
But not in the ways I can count

I love you because I lose focus in those emerald eyes
You love me because I like looking into your eyes

Burning

Fire does not ask permission.
It takes. It consumes. It becomes.
I chose not to fight fire with fire.
But choosing water does not stop the flames.
When the walls fell, they called me
Weak.
Insecure
And pathetic.
As if standing in the ruins was not enough.
I am not a victim.
but the fire takes me as such.

Clenched fist

To be loved—that's all I want.
To find a beautiful girl,
and hear her say
that I am worth seeing.
Eight billion hearts beat in this world,

Surely one could beat for me?

And yet, here I stand,
waiting,
hoping,
heart open.

Part V

There are moments in life when I think I've seen it all, felt it all, and then suddenly, I'm blindsided by the truth of my own foolishness. Well, here I am, that very downfall I sensed before, like Icarus drawn inevitably towards the radiant sun.

It all started with her—so alluring, so enchanting. I was drawn to her like a moth to a flame, knowing deep down that I would end in flames. But I couldn't resist soaring closer, blinded by her brilliance and oblivious to the impending descent into darkness.

I thought maybe, just maybe, I could change the course of fate, rewrite the ending, be able to touch the sun and feel its gentle skin, like I was the author of my own story. But I was merely a pawn in a game far, older and crueller than my naive heart could fathom.

But I've become another name on her list—a roster of broken souls she's claimed, leaving behind hollow shells like me. How foolish was I to think I could tame the sun? To believe that my love was worth the risk of burning. Now I'm just a ghost of who I once was, plummeting towards the earth and remain surrounded by my shattered dreams, still yearning for her touch.

Love Isn't Easy Anymore

Love is no longer the effortless spark it once was,
A word like *beautiful* no longer sets hearts ablaze,

Now, when I speak it, I see the dimming of light—
Not a blaze, but a flicker, slowly lost in the haze.
The word itself, once full of weight and grace,
Now floats empty, like a borrowed phrase,
Too often repeated, too hollow to claim,
Whispered too freely, bereft of flame.

I cannot call her *beautiful* without the weight of doubt,
The shadow of those I've spoken it to before,
A word too shallow, too freely tossed about,
A phrase I no longer dare to explore.

For a fleeting moment, we believe again,
We catch a glimpse of what love can be,
But how do I make her see it too,
When doubt wraps its chains around me?
How do I make my truth ring clear,
When the world around us trembles with fear?

I cannot feign indifference, I cannot be cold,
For the world has taught us to guard our hearts,
To shroud them in armor, to never be bold,
Afraid that love will tear us apart.

No one seeks love with hands wide open,
Too cautious to reach, too frightened to try.
I fear it too, this perilous thing,
But I chase, for it is only in the pursuit we win,
Failure comes not from love's attempt,
But from surrendering before we begin.

I refuse to accept that I am meant to remain,
A solitary figure, untouched by grace,
I will not let the odds decide my fate,
Not without a fight, not without a place.

Against all the evens

I wait for the secret, the cipher of love,
The map to navigate its tangled expanse,
As if there were a code to unlock this heart,
A formula, a step, a chance.
But perhaps there is no answer, no fixed road,
And perhaps the odds are skewed,

For with 8.2 billion souls on this spinning sphere,
What if one, like me, is left to brood?
They say there's someone for everyone,
But what if the universe plays tricks—
An odd number, a cosmic imbalance,
And one soul must face its fix?
Perhaps that's why I'm losing this game,
Not from lack of heart, but from fear of the same.

Instincts

That moment.
I was just standing there, across the street, waiting for the light to change.
And I saw you.
A brief glance, but you were something different.
Something that made the world pause for just a second.
"Hi. Sorry, I was just across the street, and I saw you at the traffic lights, and I thought you look absolutely beautiful."
It felt good in the moment. Felt honest.
Felt like something that could maybe brighten your day, like a little gift in a world that's too busy.

But then you said, "Thank you."
And I saw it.

Not in your eyes, but in the way your lips moved, a little too quickly, a little too flat.
Like you were disheartened, almost like you didn't believe it.
Like it wasn't true.
Did you think I was lying?
Did you think I was just saying that because it's what people say, because it's what I'm supposed to say?
Or did you think I was trying to *objectify* you?
I don't know why, but it hit me differently.
I wanted to make you feel good. I wanted to make you feel seen,
Not just some passing face, but someone worth acknowledging.
With your Big red puffy jacket and worn-out converse
But now, suddenly I'm extremely conscious of my feet in my socks in my shoes

Here I am, feeling bad.
Like I've crossed some line I didn't mean to cross.
Like my uplifting words, somehow fell flat, like stones in a pond that don't even ripple.
I guess it's just the way I was raised,
to believe in the power of words, of a compliment,
to believe that making someone feel beautiful is a kindness,
a gift you give without expecting anything in return.
But did it come out wrong?
Was I too forward?

Did it feel like I only saw you as something to be admired
instead of someone to be *known*?
Your worth knowing, Stargirl

Wonderment

I guess I just thought you'd smile,
but now I'm left wondering if I made you feel small,
if I objectified you in some way I didn't even see.
If I could take it back, I would.
Not because I think I shouldn't have said it,
but because I think I missed the chance
to show you that I see you,
really see you.
Not as some image in a moment,
but as someone with a mind, a soul,
someone beyond what's on the surface.
But I can't change it now.
All I can do is wonder:
Why does a compliment sometimes feel like a mistake?
Why does a compliment sometimes feel like an apology?

Honesty

I do not need metaphors to cloud the truth,
Nor elaborate words that twist and fade,
I seek simply to be heard, to be known,
To make her feel safe, to be unafraid.
When I say *You are the most beautiful girl I have ever seen,*
I need her to see the truth in my eyes,
To know that in her, I've found my home,
A love that's not transient, but wise.
For love is not about mastering the game,
It's about showing up, without disguise,
With open hands, with no retreat,
Saying, *I will keep trying,* despite the lies.
Saying, *I will keep believing,*
And when I say:
You are the most beautiful girl I have ever seen in my life,
I will mean it.
And I will mean it,
Every single time.

A Game of Distance

I see you.
Obvious, isn't it? The way your body moves, the way your eyes hold a moment too long.
The first thing we notice about anything is how it looks.
The first thing I noticed about you was just that.

And honestly? You're attractive.
I'd have to be blind not to notice.
It's what caught my eye, but it's not what's keeping me here.

And you remind me not to judge too quickly.
You say I don't know you.
You're right.

But everyone is a stranger before they are something more.
And I'd rather not stay a stranger to you.

You say there's no spark.
That's fine. Sparks are brief, unpredictable, gone in an instant.
But I don't chase sparks. I start fires.

You think I'm here to change your mind.
I'm not.
Your mind is already working against you.
You're still here.

Maybe you're surprised—caught off guard that someone is paying attention.
So you pause, just for a second.
And in that pause, something shifts.

The noise around us dulls, the world moves a little slower.
Not frozen, not stopped—just… quieter.
Like, for a moment, it's giving us space.

And here we are, face to face,
Still strangers, but not quite.
Something more, something undefined
Who cares
Im going to stay here as long as I can
Looking, listening, living…
the most Ive lived in a long time

Part VI

I am no god nor king,
From now on, one of the monsters, she once knew.
I held her hand and I fell in love with her, and she flew.
Another soul lost to her insatiable hunger.
As she seeks out another.
And here I sit, drowning in madness,
consumed by my one-sided lover.
Paris, goddess of my undoing
I curse you and yet I yearn you.
How cruel the gods must be to toy with mortal hearts,
To grant me love only to snatch it away.
And leave me as nothing but a shadow, left to decay.

Thank you

Kindest Regards,
Liam Campbell.

Printed in Dunstable, United Kingdom